My Best Friend
A Book About Friendship

Heather Feldman

The Rosen Publishing Group's
PowerKids Press™
New York

1

For my Mom—for being my best friend.

Published in 2000 by The Rosen Publishing Group, Inc.
29 East 21st Street, New York, NY 10010

First Edition

Book design: Danielle Primiceri

Photo Illustrations by: John Bentham; p. 22 (lollipop photo) by Thaddeus Harden.

Feldman, Heather L.
      My best friend : a book about friendship / by Heather Feldman.
      p.   cm. — (My world)
      Includes index.
      Summary: A girl describes the challenges and rewards of her
   relationship with her best friend Cindy.
      ISBN 0-8239-5526-5 (lib. bdg.)
      1. Friendship—Juvenile literature. 2. Friendship in children. [1. Best
friends. 2. Friendship.] I. Title. II. Series: Feldman, Heather L.
My world.
BF575.F66F45   1998
177'62—dc21
                                                              98-31955
                                                                   CIP
                                                                    AC

Manufactured in the United States of America

Contents

Cindy is my best friend.

5

We go to school together.

7

We have lollipops together.

9

Cindy and I like to play dress-up.

11

We like to ride our
bicycles, too.

Cindy and I always make up.

Sometimes Cindy and I don't agree with each other.

15

Cindy and I always make up.

17

When I am sad, Cindy
makes me feel better.

19

Cindy is my best friend in the whole world.

Words to Know

FRIEND

LOLLIPOP

SAD

BICYCLE

Here are more books to read about friends:
A Friend Is Someone Who Likes You
by Joan Walsh Anglund
Harcourt Brace & Co.

*How to Be a Friend: A Guide to Making
Friends and Keeping Them*
by Laurene Krasny Brown and Marc Tolon
Brown
Little, Brown & Co.

To learn more about friendship, check out these
Web sites:
http://www.edbydesign.com/storytel.html

Index

Word Count: 61

Note to Librarians, Teachers, and Parents

PowerKids Readers are specially designed to get emergent and beginning readers excited about learning to read. Simple stories and concepts are paired with photographs of real kids in real-life situations. Spirited characters and story lines that kids can relate to help readers respond to written language by linking meaning with their own everyday experiences. Sentences are short and simple, employing a basic vocabulary of sight words, as well as new words that describe familiar things and places. Large type, clean design, and photographs corresponding directly to the text all help children to decipher meaning. Features such as a picture glossary and an index help children get the most out of PowerKids Readers. Lists of related books and Web sites encourage kids to explore other sources and to continue the process of learning. With their engaging stories and vivid photo-illustrations, PowerKids Readers inspire children with the interest and confidence to return to these books again and again. It is this rich and rewarding experience of success with language that gives children the opportunity to develop a love of reading and learning that they will carry with them throughout their lives.